Next Chapter

It's Never Too Late to Transform Your Life

PEGI IVERY BROWN

Cover Design by 100Covers.com
Interior Design by FormattedBooks.com

ISBN: 978-1-7345061-1-2 (Paperback)
ISBN: 978-1-7345061-0-5 (Ebook)

FIRST EDITION

Dedication

This book is dedicated to my mother, Ann Rebecca Days. Thank you for being my original example of the Next Chapter woman. Your quiet determination to live your dream later in life is the roadmap I've followed. Thank you for the warmth and security of your love that envelops me even now. Continue to watch over me from heaven.

And to my son Derek Ivery, your love, patience and unwavering faith in me is my inspiration. Without your continued encouragement and support, I may not have finished this book. You are an amazing man and I'm honored to be your mom.

It never fails to amaze me how God uses seemingly unrelated incidents to change the trajectory of people's lives.

—Pegi Ivery Brown

Contents

Introduction

The marquee above Madison Square Garden flashed WELCOME LAGUARDIA COMMUNITY COLLEGE CLASS OF 2015. I know I was in the right place. But as a baby boomer surrounded by millennials, I felt invisible. I pushed that thought aside, knowing the crowd would swallow me up if I didn't focus on finding the end of the processional line. The streets were jam-packed with family and friends of the graduates; buying flowers, balloons, and teddy bears dressed in the school colors, to commemorate the occasion. Graduates ran back and forth, their caps and gowns fluttering in the wind as they snapped selfies with each other to capture the moment.

It was Graduation Day, but I wasn't celebrating. It was forty years too late to be making a big fuss over just one day.

Inside the arena there were several lines going in every direction to accommodate the huge crowd of graduating students, almost 1600 of us. We crept along, snaking our way through the enormous building towards the theatre where the ceremony would take place. With so many people, I assumed my family would never find me in the crowd. However, on entering the theatre, I didn't have to search through too many faces before I spotted my family standing almost directly in front of me. While I'd made a conscious decision to downplay my graduation, my family did the exact opposite.

My son Derek, my niece Jackie, and her son Little James were jumping up and down, waving their arms and screaming my name like I was a superstar and they were my fan club. Watching their excitement triggered something inside me. This wasn't just another day—it was my graduation. It was about so much more than the associate degree I was earning. It culminated a forty-year dream that I dared not share with anyone because I never thought it was even possible for me. But I'd set the goal, and even though at times I wanted to give up, I did the work, and now I was achieving my goal. This moment deserved a celebration. And not just for me, but for my family. Even beyond my family: my accomplishment was for all the people who decide to reclaim the dreams they'd allowed to slip away. Why was I dimming my light, hiding in the shadows? Because others would think it was too late for me to realize my dream? If anyone thought that, why should I care? This was my dream! I achieved it, and my age didn't matter. I proved to myself it wasn't too late, and I knew one day I'd share that message with others—that it's never too late for them either.

The commencement ceremony was a flurry of greetings, award presentations, and a few brief speeches. Then, Dr. Gail O. Mellow, the president of LaGuardia Community College, announced that each graduate—all 1600 of us—would walk across the stage and announce our name and major. While the minutes until now had flown by, they slowed to a painful crawl until they finally called my row to line up behind the stage. I'd had plenty of time to make myself crazy with thoughts of all the things that could go wrong, like tripping up the stairs or falling on the stage or opening my mouth and not being able to say anything. From backstage I could hear some students giving their team or club affiliations in their introduction. *Oh, God,* I panicked.

What will I say? "I don't belong to a club or team! I've done nothing to make myself stand out at LaGuardia!" Without a second left to figure out my intro, it was my turn. Somehow, I made my way to the mic at center stage. The bright lights in my eyes made it impossible to make out the faces in the audience which was a good thing. With my heart about to jump out of my chest, I took a deep breath and said, "I am the sixty-two-year-old communications major, Pegi Ivery Brown!" The arena erupted into applause, cheers and shouts, people standing on their feet. I stood there a few extra beats to let it soak in. If ever I had a 'drop-the-mic' moment, this was it. My age was the reason I felt invisible at college; who knew others would celebrate me for it?

Making my way back to my seat, I slapped a lot of high fives. People I didn't know gave me thumbs up and congratulatory pats on the back. Others my age, mainly parents and grandparents of graduates, not only stopped me to offer congratulations but also to say they wished they had the courage to do what I had done.

It didn't stop after my graduation day. Wherever I told my story, the conversation inevitably shifted; people would begin sharing with me the dreams they had let escape because of life circumstances or fear. They talked about how they believed it was too late for them to reach for those dreams. I know how that feels; I felt the same way myself once. So, I started telling them this: *One day I took a tiny step forward, and then another and another, until I realized it wasn't too late for my next chapter.*

In this book, I take you on a personal journey into my life's next chapter. I share how low self-esteem and self-doubt held me hostage, leaving me unable to enjoy life. You will find me open about dealing with forgiveness, self-love, depression, and fear.

Mine is not a rags-to-riches story of a person starting out poor, achieving great success, wealth or celebrity, then providing you the steps to do the same. This is an account of an ordinary woman in her fifties deciding she was tired of life passing her by. She wanted to live the dreams God placed in her heart. She took a step toward her next chapter and realized it wasn't too late.

A Message for You

It is my hope and purpose that through my story, grounded in real-life situations and lessons I learned, you will feel inspired to step towards your Next Chapter—it's never too late. At the end of each chapter in this book I've included a few thoughts for your reflection, or a quick exercise to try. I did this because while I want you to connect with my story, I also want to help you focus on your own dreams. Where are the lessons in your own life and how can they help you move forward? And if you feel stuck, examine the reasons why? At the end of the book, I've included a list of books that you might find helpful on your journey to your next chapter.

CHAPTER 1

Wake-Up Call

The year I turned fifty, Aunt Bernice, my father's youngest sister, was the oldest living relative left in the family. She always said whatever came to mind without regard for how her words might hurt. When I was little, I didn't think she liked me, and I never understood why. She made fun of my clothes being too big, my hair being too nappy and the gap in between my front teeth. Although I did my best to stay on her good side, she'd find something to complain about— like when I was eight or nine years old she cautioned me to be extra careful washing her "very expensive" china and crystal, then every five minutes she's back in the kitchen huffing and puffing telling me I was too slow. Or the time she blew a gasket when I folded the dinner napkins in triangles instead of rectangles. She snatched the remaining napkins out of my hand, shoving me to the side, while mumbling how she knew she should have done it herself because I was useless.

As a teenager it thrilled me when I no longer had to spend the first three weeks of summer vacation at grandma's house, where Aunt

Bernice and her husband also lived. Other times I used every excuse in the book to avoid her. I dread being in her presence. But somehow, God tied my destiny to hers and hers to mine.

Over time dementia claimed my aunt's mind, but not before she knew I was her legal guardian, responsible for every aspect of her life. Don't be mistaken, I didn't take on this responsibility out of the desire to perform some grand, noble gesture. I didn't do it out of love either—at least, not the kind of love where you feel warm and fuzzy toward the other person. I did it because my parents' voices droned in my head, saying, "She's family. That's what we do."

Aunt Bernice and I never talked about how she treated me as a child. However, one day, while looking through old photos together, hoping it might trigger her memory, she said in a voice just above a whisper, "I never thought it would be you." I turned to see her eyes filling with tears.

Years of anger for the way she treated me rushed back through my mind and quickly vanished like a puff of smoke. It just didn't matter anymore. Before that moment I thought for our relationship to heal, it would require an enormous display of forgiveness. Aunt Bernice would have to acknowledge all her unfairness towards me, show remorse, then ask me outright for forgiveness. She never asked for forgiveness. And yet somehow, I let it go. With the magnitude of the job of caring for her in front of me, I knew it was best to make peace with the past and allow a new relationship to form.

Over the next few years, I coordinated every area of her life, including hiring home health care attendants and later, moving her to an assisted living facility, and then a nursing home. In her last year, Aunt Bernice no longer communicated and would only grunt or moan in response to any attempt to have a conversation.

One afternoon, as I was about to leave her room at the nursing home, she said, "Don't go yet." It startled me to hear her speak. Only three words; still, it was her first complete sentence in over a year. I listened attentively.

"The man came last night, but he told me I must wait," she said.

"Wait—what man?"

"I must wait," she said again, not really responding to me, instead stating a fact into the air. This time I understood. Aunt Bernice's time was almost here. As the reality of her words sank in, the sadness followed. Her passing would mark the end of an era. A whole generation of my family would no longer be here.

Equally sad was how long she waited for this moment. When her husband passed away almost two decades earlier, she began her wait. She stopped living and started slowly dying. She waited nineteen years for her physical transition. Even before dementia took its toll, she decided to give up on life and took a seat on the sidelines, waiting to die. I watched her stop doing everything she enjoyed: church, the senior center, painting, shopping, even going into her garden. To me, it appeared she was cutting herself off from everything that resembled living.

"I must wait," would be her final words to me. She had nothing more to say. A few days later, she passed away... her wait was over.

My aunt's last words played over and over in my head: *I must wait—I must wait.* An image of a woman sitting in a drab train station formed in my mind, like in an old black-and-white TV Western. There she sat on a bench, completely still, just waiting. Through the window we can see the world in vivid colors zooming by, but she chooses to sit and wait.

I wondered if Aunt Bernice's words held a deeper meaning. Was she trying to tell me something before transitioning? Or was I trying to make something out of nothing, as we often do when people die? Perhaps there was a connection between her life and mine beyond the family DNA. I searched for an answer, but after a while concluded that there was no deeper connection. My life wasn't anything like hers.

I was super busy; my life was full of activities. I wasn't sitting around just waiting. I was living!

Or was I?

It turns out, Aunt Bernice's final words were her parting gift to me, a wake-up call. Her words prompted a major overhaul in my life.

Once Aunt Bernice was gone, I still had plenty on my calendar. But I didn't have a vision, a goal, or a plan. I realized I'd allowed low self-esteem, insecurities, and fear to paralyze me. I valued the opinions of others more than my own. With this negative self-image, I was limiting my view of what was possible for me. Even after I'd been able to let go of some old hurts as I helped Aunt Bernice, I still lived trapped in the past, rehashing mistakes; never forgiving myself or anyone else. And worst of all, life was passing me by. At fifty-plus I had missed out on so much of my own life while I sat waiting, hoping something would magically happen. I was waiting, and just like Aunt Bernice, I wasn't living... I was slowly dying.

Thankfully, I didn't get just one wake-up call. I received a series of little nudges from God, forcing me to pay attention to what was going on. Rewriting my past wasn't possible and remaining the same was not an option. I decided to stop waiting and start living. I wasn't exactly sure what that would mean, but I prepared myself to do whatever it took to make my next chapter my best chapter.

Do You Need a Wake-up Call from "Life as Usual"?

Wake-up calls sometime arrive in the form of a scary medical report, a financial crisis, the death of a loved one or some other life-altering experience. Wake-up calls alert us to things right in front of our face that we cannot see because we have grown accustomed to life as usual. We overlook problems ahead, dangers brewing, and we cannot acknowledge our dissatisfaction with things the way they are.

A wake-up call can flip your world upside down; but be grateful for the gift it brings. It is an opportunity to make a life assessment. Use the moment to give some thought to questions like:

- Am I living my best life?
- Am I taking care of my physical, mental, and spiritual needs?
- Do I have a vision for what's next? Do I have a purpose or goals?
- Or have I settled? Have I lowered my expectations because it's easier than risking failure?

You may not have answers to any of these, but at least you'll be thinking about where you are and where your life is headed. Don't judge yourself—you are where you are and that's okay. This is your wake-up call. It's your opportunity to assess your choices. It marks the end of one thing and signals the beginning of something new and beautiful.

CHAPTER 2

How Did I Get Here?

As a child I dreamt of becoming a ballerina, a nurse, and a singer—all three at the same time. But singer topped the list. I had a plan. I'd appear on the *Ted Mack Original Amateur Hour* TV Show. Long before *American Idol* and *America's Got Talent,* there was *The Original Amateur Hour*. Every Sunday evening I'd park myself in front of the television to watch contestants compete for prizes. Viewers voted by calling in or mailing in postcards. I was sure one day I'd be the winner and after a long drum roll Ted Mack would announce my name!

At eight years old, my reality was singing in the junior choir at Day Spring Baptist Church, around the corner from where I lived with my parents and older sister in Harlem. I'm not sure when I started singing; it was something I always did. Often, I'd be invited to neighborhood churches to sing for their Sunday afternoon programs. Everyone loved to hear the little girl with the grown-up voice. My parents never turned down an invitation.

They said my voice was a gift from God. As an infant I cried, but my cries were barely audible. The doctors treated me for all kinds of illnesses, and since my father had lost a lung to tuberculosis years earlier; they treated me for that as well. The doctors instructed my parents to take an adult dosage of the TB medication, divide it into four parts, then dissolve it in my formula. Truthfully, my condition baffled the doctors and they never gave my parents a medical explanation for it.

Three years before I was born, my brother Bobby had died suddenly and without a clear cause. Naturally, my parents were concerned something life threatening might be wrong with me. Being people of faith, they prayed continuously for my healing, but nothing seemed to happen. Then one day I let out an ear-piercing cry and that was the end of that. Singing, my parents told me, was my opportunity to honor God by giving back to Him what He had given me.

The Junior Jubilees was a group of young people ages eight to eighteen that sang gospel music throughout the city and occasionally were featured on local radio. I idolized everything about the group, from their fancy choir robes to the way they swayed back and forth when they sang. But they were way out of my league, the thought of singing with them never crossed my mind.

When I heard they were coming to my church for our choir anniversary program, I was beside myself. The minute they arrived I began following them around the church like a little stalker. They mesmerized me, I tried to soak in their every move. When it was their turn to sing, it was better than I could have imagined. They sang four or five songs; more than the usual two numbers most guest choirs sing. Their voices blended in perfect harmony as they sang all types of sacred music from hymns to spirituals and contemporary gospel. I could have listened to them all afternoon, but our own choir was coming up next to end the program.

As always, I was one of the lead vocalists. When it was my turn, I put a little extra something on top of my usual singing. I heard myself doing vocal gymnastics, ad-libbing and doing riffs seemingly out of nowhere. I walked up and down the aisle, throwing my head back and gesturing with my hands like I'd seen older, more experienced singers do. I wasn't showing off; the Junior Jubilees inspired me to give my best. Maybe I was showing off a little bit, caught up in the moment.

When we got home that evening, my parents called me into their room. I thought I was in big trouble for my antics at church. But no— instead they told me the director of the Junior Jubilees was interested in me joining the group. She'd heard me sing a few times before but thought I was too young back then. Now she felt the time was right. She extended an invitation for me to audition. By "audition" she meant to test my vocal range to determine where I would fit in the group. My spot was secure if my parents said yes.

After a silent moment to grasp what I was hearing, I went wild screaming, jumping up and down. "Yes, yes," I shouted, "The Junior Jubilees want me!" I made it into a song. "The Junior Jubilees want me... the Junior Jubilees want me."

As I danced around the room, I realized I wouldn't be needing *Ted Mack's Original Amateur Hour* anymore. I would be a Junior Jubilee. In all my celebrating, I failed to notice the frozen expression on my parents' faces. Their decision was already NO.

My heart broke into a million pieces. I tried to argue that it wasn't fair; the lady said she wanted me. "She wants me to be a Junior Jubilee!" I screamed at the top of my voice.

Mommy shot me one of those looks that black mothers used to give their children in church back in the day when they crossed the line, or it looked as if they were about to. In that moment, I didn't care. I struck a pose with my chest poked out, huffing and puffing. But I knew it was case closed. I stood in complete silence as the tears rolled down my face. My shoulders sagged; I dropped my pose. I knew better than debate the issue any further.

Meanwhile Mommy and Daddy continued talking to each other as if I wasn't in the room, about people they knew that ruined their lives chasing careers in show business. I didn't understand what that had to do with me, so I came to my own conclusion why they said no. I assumed my parents didn't think I was good enough to sing with a group like the Junior Jubilees. All that talk about my voice being a gift from God, well, that was just talk.

No matter the number of solos I had at church or invitations to sing at neighborhood churches, it was never the same after that big disappointment. That night my dream died, along with the belief that my voice was a gift from God.

Singing was my strong suit, the one place I excelled without worries of whether I was good enough or smart enough. I needed a place to feel good about myself to compensate for feeling inferior everywhere else. Singing was my safe space. Without it, all I had was school, where I felt anything but special.

School was my own personal hell. Everything in school hinges on your ability to read, and I wasn't a very good reader. It was especially frustrating because it seemed to come naturally to everyone else. I believed I was just plain dumb. It didn't help that Cooki, my sister, and my best friend Sherrie were both exceptional students. My sister even skipped a grade and Sherrie went to a special academy for gifted students. That only made it more obvious there was something wrong with me.

Parent-teacher conferences were all pretty much the same. It did not matter that I was always an enthusiastic participant in the school science fair; it did not matter I was usually the first to volunteer whenever the teacher needed help during or after class; it did not matter that I memorized every word and stage direction to every class production—eventually my teachers usually got around to saying some version of, "Pegi doesn't apply herself. She needs to try harder."

Oh, really, that's the answer—try harder?

I was trying hard; I was giving it my best. When one teacher suggested I practice reading at home Mommy and Daddy turned to the Bible, literally. Every night I had to read passages from the King James Version of the Bible. You know the one that says things like "Fret not thyself because of evildoers, neither be thou envious against the workers of iniquity"? Any person I knew would just say, "Never envy the wicked!" like the more down-to-earth Living Bible puts it. Every night I sat staring at pages filled with *thee, thy,* and *thou,* and words I couldn't pronounce or understand. It did nothing to help my reading and everything to reinforce my belief that I wasn't very smart.

Years later when my son was in second grade, he was already showing the same signs of a struggle with reading that I had growing up. Afraid he would lose his enthusiasm for learning, I reached out for help. They diagnosed Derek with a learning disability: dyslexia. Dyslexia among other things makes identifying speech sounds and learning how they relate to letters and words extremely difficult. Dyslexia often runs in families. According to the International Dyslexia Association, forty-nine percent of parents with children who have the disorder have it themselves.

Finding my reading challenges had no relations to lower intelligence was a relief. But that information came too late. I had long ago developed a strong dislike for reading. Especially the Bible.

Let Go of the Old Story

Much of what we think about ourselves starts in childhood. Children are sponges, readily absorbing whatever comes their way. They have no way of differentiating opinion from fact or the truth from fiction. Everything they take in, positive or negative, impacts on how they view themselves.

As an adult, I can look back and see that by not allowing me to join the Jubilees, my parents were probably trying to protect me.

When my Dad was young, he sang with a quartet that traveled around the South. He never shared much about that time in his life other than to say the music industry was a hard business.

Kahlil Gibran, a writer and poet, wrote about parents and their children saying, "You may give them your love but not your thoughts, for they have their own thoughts." Daddy's experience in music was his; I wish they gave me the opportunity to have my own. Or at least know the reason they said no to me, so I didn't have room to make up a story that stifled my dream. Instead, without realizing it, they projected their fears onto me, and from then on, I doubted myself. Self-doubt and insecurity seeped into other areas of my life, too, and affected how I saw myself well into adulthood.

What about you?

- How do you see yourself?
- How do you think others' opinions of what you could become and what you could achieve shaped your self-image?
- Are there stories or negative thoughts you need to let go of to start your next chapter?

Before you move forward into your next chapter, it's important that you reflect on how you arrived at who you are today. You may have put limitations on what was possible for you to achieve based on words from a well-meaning parent, teacher, trusted authority figure, or friend. You created a story around something said years ago because you valued their opinion of you and your dreams more than your own. And you repeated the story to yourself so often it rang true. Or perhaps you limited yourself by comparing yourself to others. Too often we compare our weakness to others' strength, which will always create a story we are not good enough. Whatever the story however created, if it's not propelling you forward into your best life, it's time to let it go.

Don't look back in despair. Don't worry about the time wasted. Don't wish for an opportunity to do it all over. The past is the past. You cannot rewrite it. But you have the power to write your next chapter and fill it with new hopes, dreams, and a world of new possibilities.

CHAPTER 3

Time for a Change

School did not get easier, but I always met the minimum requirements to move to the next grade. High school presented a new set of challenges along with just enough freedom to get myself in trouble. To avoid the crushing embarrassment I'd inevitably suffer in the classroom—being drilled on homework I hadn't completed or getting called on to read out loud—I'd chill out in the girls' room smoking cigarettes and hiding from the hall monitor.

My girls and I would hang in the park drinking Boones Farm Apple Wine, Mad Dog 20/20 or any other cheap wine we bought with money we hustled up. We'd go to the cafeteria and wait outside the cashier's booth for the most easygoing kids and beg for the loose change on their trays after they paid for their meal. We never asked for more than what we needed to get our next bottle, and then we were out of there and back to the park.

Occasionally a bunch of us would jump the turnstile and head into Manhattan on the #7 train to terrorize the streets of the East Village.

Running in and out of those funky little shops along McDougal and Bleecker Street, we'd snatch love beads and other trinkets off the counters—whatever we got our hands on. Except for the occasional junk food, most of the stuff we stole ended up in the trash. We were just having fun. Anything was better than being in school.

Then one day police caught my friends and took them in handcuffs to the precinct. They had to stay in custody until their parents arrived. Thank God I had the flu and was home sick that day or else I would have been right alongside them. The thought of my parents getting a call from the police still gives me chills all these decades later. It was enough to bring an abrupt end to my life of crime.

My attitude toward school changed quickly, mostly because of the police incident but also because of the "graduation in doubt" notifications that Flushing High School kept sending home. Surely my parents would follow through on their threat to put my "narrow behind on the curb with my suitcase" if they got one more.

I didn't turn into a straight-A student, but my attendance improved. And when I was in class, I tried hard to focus. I found I enjoyed the marketing and business administration classes and I even excelled in accounting.

When everyone began talking about college, I got caught up in the excitement. I filled out an application for LaGuardia Community College, a new addition to the City University of New York campus in the early 1970s. But I didn't go.

My application was not rejected. I never mail it in.

It took five years instead of four to graduate high school, but I had my diploma and I was finished with school. No more anxiety about taking tests or writing papers. I was free. I was sure those challenges would not exist for me in the real world.

Could I possibly hate anything more than I hated school? Yes: my first job. I was a file clerk with an insurance company. When the elevator doors opened that first day all I could see in every direction was row after row of file cabinets. All day, every day, I took files out and put files back. The repetition was mind numbing. Within a few weeks I reverted to my high school play book of disappearing when I felt challenged. I began playing hooky from work. They fired me in no time.

I learned quickly that the work world was not like high school and I'd better get it together. Next, I found a position in the accounting department of one of the top advertising agencies in the world. Doyle Dane Bernbach, internationally known as DDB, was revolutionary for its time, infusing humor in their ad campaigns. One of their best known was the Alka-Seltzer "Mamma Mia, that's-a one spicy meatball" commercial. They helped to popularize the unconventionally designed Volkswagen Beetle, leading to a surge in its import numbers to the U.S. The atmosphere at DDB was in complete contrast to the drab, morgue-like surroundings at the insurance company. It was bright and cheerful with lots of open space and giant posters of recent ad campaigns lining the walls. It was a fun and lively environment, with celebrities coming in and out. Clients and representatives from TV, radio, and print media outlets sent goodie bags, invites to parties, and tickets to Broadway shows and sporting events. Management provided incentives and perks like two-hour lunches, discounts on clients' products, and frequent half-day Fridays, which helped to counterbalance the high volume of fast-paced work.

Where I lacked confidence in other areas, I more than made up for it when dealing with numbers. Accounting was my comfort zone. In less than a year I became the assistant supervisor for the print media accounts payable group. It was my responsibility to ensure our group processed all the newspaper, billboard, consumer and trade magazines' invoices to meet the deadlines. This was before computers and email, so sometimes I'd have to physically walk to other departments to resolve issues for one of my clients or to help someone in my group. That's how I meet John Brancaccio. John was a senior estimator in the media department. He was a big guy who reminded me of Hardy from the Laurel and Hardy comedy duo. John was an easygoing guy with a sense of humor as big as he was, which made working with him the opposite of intimidating. We worked together on many of the agency's regional clients, which were the most challenging. Each area had a different set of guidelines to consider when reserving space for ads and processing payments. John said I had a knack for dealing with the smaller media outlets and the patience he didn't have to walk them through the process. I just knew the feeling of overwhelm being handed a stack of unfamiliar papers and not being able to navigate the language or the process, so I did my best to eliminate that feeling for our vendors whenever I could.

When an opening came up in the media department, John recommend me for the spot. It was a media estimator position and would involve preparing estimates for the client and issuing contracts for space in print media outlets. What terrified me the most was communicating with planners, buyers, the account executive group, and possibly clients by writing letters and memos to them. Never in a million years would I have applied for the position on my own. Although I had developed ways to compensate for my reading and writing challenges, I still felt insecure and anxious about both. Numbers were my thing. If I stayed in Accounting, I knew I'd be okay.

I listened as John gave me all the details about the position. While he talked, I searched for an excuse to turn down this new position. I couldn't tell him what I was really thinking—that I wasn't smart enough. So, I said nothing. I left it in the hands of management. I was sure they'd eliminate me from the pool of qualified applicants. I had neither the college degree nor the experience required for the position.

John must have done one heck of a sales job on my behalf with the media director. Without an interview or even a conversation, they offered me the position, which included a nice salary increase. All they needed was my decision. If I said no, I'd look like an idiot for turning down a great opportunity. But if I said yes, I might set myself up for failure. I grappled with the decision for days. Not knowing how to get out of it, I said yes.

After accepting the position, I was scared. What if I couldn't handle the responsibility? What if I had to read something that I didn't understand in front of people? What if I let John down? My "what ifs" were endless. In client meetings I never took notes, afraid someone might see them. I rarely asked questions, thinking people might think I was stupid for not understanding. If anyone asked for clarity on one of my projects, I'd sweat and squirm. Easily intimidated, I always assumed I was in error. I worried the next person through the door or on the phone would realize I was in over my head.

Fear and insecurity ruled both my personal and professional life. I was afraid if people got to know me, they wouldn't like me, so I hid my feelings and opinions on just about everything. I said yes when I wanted to say no and no to things that, in my heart, I really wanted to say yes to. I measured myself against others by my limitations, totally ignoring all my good qualities. I always felt like I was pretending I was someone I was not. I was a fake, a phony, and a fraud.

Being me was totally exhausting. All the hiding and pretending was draining the life out of me. I didn't want to continue living that way, and one day I decided I wouldn't anymore. I wasn't a helpless victim—I had the power to choose how I wanted to be in the world. It was time for a change.

Decide. Act. Change.

After high school and out in the world, I didn't think very highly of myself. Because of how I saw myself, I didn't value what I had to offer. I applied for jobs like the one at the insurance company because they would not be too demanding or require much from me intellectually. My expectations were low, so I aimed low and settled for far less than what I was worth. And even when I landed a great position (thanks to someone who knew my work well!), I still suffered from impostor syndrome, living in constant fear I'd expose myself as a fraud.

One day I had enough. I grew tired of living life that way. When you feel like that, it's time for a change. Tony Robbins said, "Change happens when the pain of staying the same is greater than the pain of change." And the good news, change is simple. It begins with a decision. When you decide to change there is a shift in your thinking and your belief in what is possible. There's no evidence anything is happening right away, but you've gone from wishing and hoping something could be different to deciding not to remain the same.

After the decision, change will also require action. There is a story in the Bible of a man who was an invalid for thirty-eight years. Jesus sees the man lying beside a pool called Bethesda in Jerusalem. They said the pool had healing powers for the first person to enter it after an angel stirs the water. Jesus asks the man a question: "Do you want to get well?" It seems a strange question. You might think, *with all due respect Jesus, the dude's been sitting there for thirty-eight years. Anyone would want to get well after that much suffering.* But we cannot assume, just because he's been lying there, that he wants to change his circumstances. Maybe he's given up hope that things could be different. Maybe he's filled with disappointments. Or perhaps he thinks it's too late for a change. Jesus challenges the man to take action, radical action. He says, "Get up, pick up your mat, and walk." And the man takes action and walks.

To get a different result, we must do something different. Change will happen when we find the courage to get in action.

When you decide it's time for a change, accept that it will not all happen overnight. Change is a process. Small steps taken one after another over time will eventually lead you where you want to go. Don't get discouraged and don't give up. You'll get there.

Take some time to consider these questions:

- Are you sick and tired of settling for less than life has to offer you?
- What would your life look like if you changed?
- What's holding you back from taking action now?

CHAPTER 4

Journey to God

G rowing up a PK—preacher's kid—isn't easy. Besides your parents, the whole church congregation has their eyes on you. Church folk can be some of the nosiest, most judgmental people on earth. They watch your every move, ready to pounce on the slightest indiscretion while keeping score of every mistake. They think the African proverb "it takes a village to raise a child" entitles them to voice their opinion on how you dress, what you do, where you go and who your friends should be. They hold you to a much higher standard than they hold themselves or their own bad-behind kids.

As adults, many PKs follow their parents' footsteps into the pulpit or some other leadership role in the church. But I've also observed others march right down the center aisle straight out the back door, finally free, never returning, or at least not for a very long time. Still others, like me, find ourselves stuck in church limbo—neither fully in nor fully out, just going through the motions.

My Dad, or Pastor Days as he was known to the world, entered ministry later than most at age forty-five. His devotion to God and the church was beyond my comprehension. He spent hours each day studying, reading scripture, praying, preparing for Bible study, prayer meeting, and Sunday worship service, not to mention his other pastoral duties. Pastors are on call twenty-four-seven.

Until I was twelve, our family lived on the second floor of a brownstone in Harlem. Our neighbor had the front room and we were in the back. We all shared the same bathroom in the hallway, including the tenant who lived on the first floor. Our apartment was actually one large room divided down the middle with a paper-thin wall to give the appearance of two rooms. When my sister and I got home from school, we'd turn the TV on with the volume just above mute to avoid disturbing Daddy, who was always studying on the other side of the wall. With the TV volume down that low sometimes it was hard to figure out what was going on in our shows. But having the TV on made us feel like regular kids.

When your father is the pastor, church becomes the family business. Daddy often quoted Joshua 24:15, "…as for me and my household, we will serve the Lord." And that's exactly what we did. Mommy as First Lady was also the missionary advisor and Sunday school teacher. She was on the usher board, sang in the choir, and sometimes filled in as church secretary.

My sister and I went to Sunday school, vacation Bible school, and religious training (which I didn't mind because we got to leave school early on Wednesday afternoons to attend). Then we had the junior choir, junior ushers, junior stewardesses, junior officers, and either BTU—Baptist Training Union when we attended the Baptist church—or YPD, Young People's Department, when we returned home to the African Methodist Episcopal Church.

Since Cooki played the piano, and I sang, the Days Sisters were always available for any type of program, including funerals and weddings. Sunday was a marathon: 9:00 a.m. Sunday school, 11:00 a.m. morning worship service. Someone was always selling dinners between services downstairs in the dining hall. Then at 3:30, everyone came back upstairs for the afternoon program. Occasionally there was a 6:00 evening service too.

Friday nights, while most kids were chilling out after a long week at school, I was at church on my knees at prayer meeting. Saturday after weekly chores, it was time for choir rehearsal. As if that weren't enough, Monday through Thursday evening the minute the dinner dishes were put away, Daddy would call out, "Get your Bibles." It was time for family Bible study. Those sessions seemed to drag on forever. I'd sit there daydreaming or wondering what was happening on TV and hoping Daddy would forget to call on me to read out loud, knowing the torture that would bring for us all. Our family was all church all the time. I couldn't wait to grow up and leave church life behind.

However, when I was old enough to leave, I didn't. I didn't stay out of a personal commitment to God or church; I was in limbo–stuck. I stayed because of my conditioning. Pop culture says it takes twenty-one days to develop a habit. Scientific research puts it somewhere between eighteen and 254 days. Whichever is true, imagine how ingrained a routine can be after twenty-plus years.

When my first marriage dissolved, I slowly drifted away from church. My ex-husband wasn't much of a churchgoer when we met. But by the time we separated he had become so heavily entrenched in every aspect of the church life and leadership that his absence left an obvious void. It was easier for me to walk away than deal with questions from gossiping church people or tolerate the awkwardness of conversations abruptly ending when I entered the room.

With church on the back burner, my world revolved around raising my son and going to work. Mergers and corporate takeovers were happening so fast and furious in the advertising industry it was hard to keep track. Management teams changed with every new acquisition. Sometimes overnight, we found ourselves reporting to a different director. This time we ended up with one who clearly was not pleased how things turned out for her, and her attitude showed it.

MaryAnne Lansburgh was in her fifties, never married, with no children, and had dedicated her life to getting ahead in her career. She rose to Senior Vice President Associate Media Director in a male-dominated industry. MaryAnne had lost most of her previous staff as casualties of the last round of layoffs when her agency merged with ours. She was notorious for assigning projects with specific instructions, then within hours of her deadline she'd completely change the scope of the project without warning or explanation. She wouldn't extend her original deadline to accommodate the last-minute changes. She was in the habit of scheduling staff meetings fifteen minutes before close of day and complain because people were watching the clock instead of focusing on whatever tirade she was on at the moment.

Her erratic management style pushed most of her team to the limits of their patience, and the rest of them out the door in search of other opportunities.

On the way to work one morning, I replayed in my mind the drama from the previous day and knew more of the same would be waiting for me when I arrived at the office. I felt the full force of the stress I was under come down on me. In the past I could turn it off like an on-off switch, but not this time. I could not find the strength. I knew that by admitting I couldn't handle it any more, MaryAnne would see that as a weakness and go all in making my life at work more unbearable. The only solution I saw was to resign.

But I couldn't quit my job without having another one lined up—I had my little boy depending on me. Scared and afraid I didn't know what to do.

Standing there trying to figure out my next move, a scripture I'd memorized as a child popped into my head: "Do not be anxious about anything, but in every situation, by prayer and petition, with thanksgiving, present your requests to God. And the peace of God, which transcends all understanding, will guard your hearts and your minds…"

And then I thought, *I've tried everything else. Let me try this God stuff Daddy believes so strongly in.* In the middle of morning rush hour on a crowded New York City subway platform, I reached out to God. With tears streaming down my face, I admitted I couldn't handle the job situation by myself and said, "God, please help me." Then I stepped onto the train. That simple prayer was the beginning of my spiritual journey to finding God.

As the train ascended out of the tunnel onto the elevated tracks over the city, a feeling of peace washed over me. I don't know how I knew, but I was sure everything would be all right. The fear and anxiety left, replaced with a confidence that whatever came my way, I'd be able to handle it. For the first time in a long time I walked down Madison Avenue toward the office with a smile on my face. I was at peace.

I wish I could say MaryAnne became a rational, considerate person because of my prayer, but that did not happen. If anything, she got worse. My prayer didn't change her, but it changed me and my attitude toward her. Her actions no longer had the same effect. I saw things in a different light and my compassion towards her grew.

Praying in the middle of a subway station meltdown caused a major shift in my life. Since leaving the church, I hadn't given my relationship with God much thought. Now I wondered what connecting with Him regularly would mean. I wanted to maintain the feeling of peace in my life, so I tried it. Each morning before work I set aside a few moments to pray. I noticed a change. It was as if a heaviness I had felt for years was slowly lifting. Still, I wondered if my simple morning prayers meant I was in relationship with God. My prayer time didn't resemble in length or intensity what I'd witnessed my father do. I worried I wasn't doing it right.

The last months before Daddy passed away, he was in and out of the hospital. Right up to the end we could still depend on him for two things: telling corny jokes, and unapologetically sharing his love for God with everyone. On more than one occasion I arrived at the hospital during shift changes to find him praying with Numayra, a nurse who I knew to be of a different faith. It puzzled me and after a while I said, "Daddy, you do know that Numayra is not a Christian?" I watched a little smile spread across his face as if he was amused by my naivety. He said, "No single religion has the exclusive rights to God." Wait a minute, was that my father the AME preacher talking? Then he added, "Everyone has a right to believe in something." Daddy's words seemed contrary to what I assumed he believed about God, but they were in total alignment with who I was finding God to be.

My view of God expanded beyond the constraints of the religious box we tend to place Him in. God is limitless and bigger than religion. He is more available, more approachable, more accepting than I ever could have imagined.

I realized that, for me, a relationship with God was essential, not only for my spiritual well-being, but also for my mental and physical well-being. Positive psychology research shows that having a connection to a higher power is beneficial to one's overall good health. People with a faith-based or spiritual foundation are proven to experience more happiness, live longer, have lower rates of stress and depression, sleep better, achieve higher academically, and enjoy better mental health.

Our relationship with God is the foundation of our spiritual life. I love the way Pierre Teilhard de Chardin, French Philosopher and Jesuit priest, put it when he said, "We are spiritual beings having a human experience." For me, spending time with God is an opportunity to connect back to my spiritual source. I like to think of it as connecting spirit to spirit, joining as one. Connecting back to the source of infinite power. Like when we charge our phones—we're replenishing the power that was lost. When we spend time with God, we are restoring power back to ourselves from our source.

While rediscovering God I found on my bookshelf, in the original packaging, a Bible given to me in my early twenties by Pastor William D. Watley, PhD. Written in contemporary English, it was easy for me to read and understand. I thought, *if this was the Bible we used during those family Bible study sessions, I may not have drifted off so much!* It surprised me that with all the time I spent in church growing up, how little I really knew about God. I wanted to know more.

Eventually I returned to church to reconnect with my spiritual family. Now it was by choice, not routine or habit. I wanted to deepen my understanding of God, and I wanted to do it inside the perimeters of the black church experience. I've worshipped in Baptist, Presbyterian, Lutheran, and non-denominational churches and I'm sure I will again but it was a cultural preference to return home to the African Methodist Episcopal Church. The AME church with its rich heritage, birthed out of the desire for equality in worship and at the forefront of social justice. The AME church a place where I could be me around a group of people just like me. My familiarity with and appreciation for the many rituals and traditions of the AME church allow me the freedom of self-expression and full involvement in the "worship experience".

I love the call-and-response style of preaching where the congregation talks back to the minister with an "Amen", "Hallelujah," or "You know that's right, Pastor." Then of course there's the music, whether thumping rhythms that make you tap your feet or jump out your seat, clapping your hands while swaying back and forth. Or the soothing sweet melodies that seem to envelop you with loving arms. In those moments I listen to the same words that brought strength and comfort to my ancestors as they dealt with far greater adversities than I must endure. This is my spiritual foundation where I am home.

Making the Connection

Examining my relationship with God as a part of my journey to my next chapter was so important because church had always played such a significant role in my life. As a child I knew church, but I didn't know God, not in a personal one-on-one way. Spending time with God and allowing that connection to grow and evolve has empowered me on my journey.

Many of us make connecting with our Divine Creator far more complicated than it needs to be. We waste time comparing, measuring or judging our prayer life based on what we think others are doing. If that's you, let go of your preconceived ideas of what it should be like. With a sincere heart and a desire to have a relationship with God, allow yourself the freedom to create a connection that is uniquely your own. Set the atmosphere in a way that speaks to your soul. Saturate your heart and mind with scriptures, inspirational writings, prayers and music that will usher you into the presence of God.

The things I may find meaningful may be different for you, and that's okay. It's more important we connect with God regularly than it is we follow a set of rules telling us how to make the connection. Some of us get so hung up on rules or rituals tied to religion that we lose sight of God. We mistakenly believe committing to religion is the same as committing to God. Yes, the structure and form our religion takes can be a beautiful and comforting expression of our beliefs and a vehicle that will lead to a better understanding of God. But our one-on-one relationship with God is far more important than which religious association we choose. Our relationship with God is as individual as we are and should be reflected in our commitment to spending time together.

Set aside some quiet time to reflect on these questions:

- Can you recall a time when you felt powerless and spiritually drained?
- Do you have a connection to God that is uniquely your own?
- Have you established a daily spiritual practice to recharge and feed your soul?

CHAPTER 5

Forgive Me — Forgive You

Barely in my twenties, I thought I knew everything about everything or at least more than my parents. I wanted out of their house, away from their rules. Marriage seemed like a good idea. Since Calvin asked, and I didn't think I could make it on my own, I said yes. He was my get-out-of-jail-free card, and maybe I was his too. Neither of us had a clue about being married, but we jumped into the lifetime commitment, anyway.

Calvin was smart, self-confident, and dependable—just what I needed to keep me grounded. When we got married, he was a college student, and I was grateful he planned to share his bright future with me. We agreed I'd be the main breadwinner while Calvin focused his attention on finishing his accounting degree. He would work part time when it didn't interfere with his class schedule. I wasn't crazy about having so much responsibility on my shoulders, but it was the sensible thing to do with only one or two years until he graduated. I figured my hard work and sacrifice up front would be my contribution to our future.

Keeping us afloat on my small salary turned out to be hard. When our one- or two-year plan stretched into its fourth year, the pressure got to me. When would I get to enjoy life instead of just working to make ends meet? As much as I disliked it, I thought I was doing what I had to do for our future. Unequipped to share my feelings, I suppressed them as best I could, not wanting Calvin to think I lost faith in him or belief in our original plan.

But suppressed emotions don't go away. I grew depressed and sometimes when he wasn't around, I'd explode in fits of rage over the slightest issue, slamming doors and breaking dishes. Once, after a disagreement about the color of our curtain rods, I went from zero to a thousand on the rage meter. The more I thought I was right, and he was wrong, the rage continued to build up inside me. Instead of my usual broken dish or slammed door, this time I was completely out of control. I tore through our bedroom, throwing things around the room like a madwoman. I started knocking things off the dresser. I flipped over the jewelry box, make-up tray, and perfume bottles, sending them tumbling to the floor. I dragged my arm across the top of the dresser causing everything left up there, including the huge mirror, to come crashing down.

The sound of the mirror shattering on the floor snapped me back to reality. I stood looking around at the mess I'd created and realized this wasn't a movie set. There was no crew coming in to clean up my mess.

Until now I thought I managed to keep my emotional outburst secret from Calvin but the aftermath of this one was difficult to explain. I think he knew but wasn't equipped to deal with whatever was going on with me. It was less complicated to let it blow over.

When Calvin went to work full time, I thought that was the end of all our problems. We'd have a normal life, the one I dreamt of and worked toward. We could finally afford things most people took for granted, like furniture, nice clothes, a vacation maybe. I was eager to start our family. Calvin reluctantly agreed to become a father.

Our son was born, and I loved every minute of being a mom. Almost immediately I noticed a change in Calvin's behavior, though. He became obsessed with jogging. He bought a bunch of new clothes and started drowning himself in Halston Z-14 every time he walked out the door. Friday night became his hang out time with the guys from work. He'd stay out until 3:00 a.m. sometimes. I knew something was wrong. I felt a distance growing between us, but Calvin assured me everything was just fine.

One day I found a letter that described in graphic detail an intimate relationship Calvin was having. At first, it didn't register. Then I realized the letter was from the Italian woman from his office who had brought a gift to the house when our baby was born. I reread the same sentences over and over, trying to make the words mean something other than Calvin was involved with her.

I felt my heart pounding in my chest. I couldn't catch my breath. To keep from falling, I lowered myself onto the bed in slow motion. The paper shook in my hands. What was I reading? It made little sense. Although in the pit of my stomach I knew it was true, I had to hear it from his mouth. I picked up the phone to call his office. As I listened to the phone ringing, I closed my eyes and tensed my whole body as if that would somehow shield me from what was about to change my life forever. Without an apology or remorse, he confirmed what I read was true. Then he added, "I love her, and I'll never give her up." It wasn't enough that he was unfaithful—he had fallen in love with her and easily told me so.

I immediately started wondering what I was lacking to make this happen. I didn't know how to be a wife. Maybe if I knew how to communicate better. Maybe if I was more this and less that. A few days later Calvin tried to walk back on his comment about loving her, but I couldn't unhear the first version. He assured me he didn't want out of the marriage. And neither did I. I wanted another chance to do things right, although I wasn't sure what that meant. Besides, I still didn't think I was strong enough to make it on my own; I needed to be married. Calvin refused any discussion about marriage counseling. He felt everything should go back to the way it was. I should trust him again without him doing anything to rebuild the trust he broke. He also wanted to remain friends with the woman. He said he was more than capable of going back to a strictly platonic relationship with her, and I had no reason for concern because he gave his word that nothing else would happen.

The innocence of our marriage was broken. Like Humpty Dumpty's great fall, all the king's horses and all the king's men couldn't put it back together again. I tried holding on to it, tried to make it work on some level, but I watched myself, turned into someone I didn't recognize. I went from wife to detective—listening in on phone calls, checking his pockets, showing up places unannounced. I became someone I didn't want to be, someone I didn't like. Calvin did absolutely nothing to relieve my anxiety. He seemed more concerned with maintaining his "friendship" than restoring our marriage.

In my heart, I knew it was over. Each time we argued I felt more betrayed, more disrespected, and more rejected. My fear of going it alone had me trapped in a marriage that was killing me inside, but I didn't have the courage to walk away. I suggested marriage counseling again, and to my surprise, this time Calvin agreed. The morning of our appointment he announced, "I'll go, but nobody's going to tell me who my friends can be." His words poured like ice water down my spine. What the hell was I hanging on to? I had enough!

There was nothing left to protect, no reason to hide anymore. I told Mommy everything. Hearing myself talk was like living it all over again—the humiliation, rejection, and betrayal. My tears turned into sobbing. At this point, I just wanted Mommy to tell me what I wanted to do was the right thing. She listened without interruption, giving me the time I needed to get it all out, and for the first time in a long time I felt relieved.

Mommy told me I was stronger than I thought, and I'd survive. Then she said, "I can't tell you what to do—that's up to you and Calvin. Whatever you decide, I've got your back one hundred percent. If you want to come home, bring the baby and you come home." Somehow, I knew I'd be okay. I wasn't sure how, but Mommy convinced me I would be, and I held on to that.

For me, the marriage was over. I had nothing left to give. I wanted out. I was at peace with my decision after talking with Mommy. She had my back. The next morning, I told Calvin I wanted a divorce.

"Are you sure?" he said in a sarcastic tone. Without giving me a chance to respond, he continued, "Cause when the tape is played back, I want it to show that you're the one that ended this thing." *Ended this thing* rang in my ears. That's what he thought of our marriage? The hours, days, weeks I'd agonized over what to do and to him it was just a thing? I don't know what I expected, but his comment caught me off guard, and I braced myself for whatever came next... but that was it. Calvin began whistling along to the music on the radio. I stood staring at him, wondering how I allowed myself to stay in it so long.

Three weeks later Mommy had a massive heart attack and died. She passed the Thursday before Thanksgiving, but it was Easter week when my emotions finally caught up with me. I hadn't cried at all over her passing until I started thinking about taking Derek to see her in his new Easter suit. Then it hit me—Mommy's gone. Everything I'd bottled up for five months came rushing back like a tsunami. As the reality that I'd never see my mother again hit home, the pain of being without her quickly became unbearable. I lay crying in my bed for hours at a time, getting up only long enough to care for Derek.

Without realizing it, I had stifled all my emotions. Not only the emotions associated with the loss of my mother, but also the feelings I had about the end of my marriage. I'd managed to shut down this part of myself for months, but now I was struggling to handle it. Mommy said I was strong; I'd need that strength more than ever now to face life all alone.

Adjusting to my new life would have been so much easier if I didn't have to deal with Calvin. Not dealing with him was impossible because we had a child to raise together. I never regretted my decision to end the marriage, but I wanted Calvin to show remorse for his actions. He never apologized for the way things turned out, nor did he admit any wrongdoing. Calvin never asked for forgiveness, and I planned never to forgive him—he did not deserve my forgiveness.

After overhearing another one of our senseless arguments, my friend Rosemary said, "Pegs, it's time to let it go. You've got to forgive him and move on." Rosemary's advice was usually right on point, but this time I thought she'd lost her mind. "Rosemary," I said, "You know what he did…" and I prepared to rehash the drama she'd heard a thousand times before.

Rosemary ignored my rant and continued her thought: "Forgive him and get on with your life. Holding on to all that stuff is only hurting you." I wondered what she was talking about. Why should I forgive him? He created this mess and never apologized. How was I supposed to let go of that? I felt justified in holding on to the anger. It was my right because of what he did and the way he did it. I would never forgive him. It took years for me to understand what Rosie was trying to teach me about forgiveness.

My concept of forgiveness had evolved little from what I learned in childhood. Someone says, "I'm sorry" and you say, "I forgive you," and just like that all is forgiven. Playtime resumes with everyone friends again. As an adult, I had to let go of my childhood idea of forgiveness to embrace what it means to truly forgive.

Before I could forgive anyone else in my life, I had to first forgive myself. For years I held on to the guilt and shame of past mistakes and poor choices. But I learned that no matter how long I held on—reliving the past, mentally beating myself up—it could never change the outcome. It was time to release myself, forgive, and move on.

Through the years Calvin and I developed a friendly relationship as we co-parented our son, but just below the surface I still held a lot of anger, resentment, and hurt from the marriage. As I began to understand the meaning of forgiveness, I realized, for my well-being and inner healing, it was time to let it go. First, I acknowledged and forgave myself for the mistakes I made during our marriage. And then, without an apology or admission of guilt from Calvin, I forgave him too. Years later Calvin took responsibility for his part in the breakup of our marriage. But by that time, I had already let it go and moved on.

Forgiveness Is for You

Forgiveness is a decision we make to release ourselves from the hurt and pain of the past. Neil Farber wrote in *Psychology Today* that "forgiveness does not happen spontaneously; it is a conscious choice to forgive." When we allow ourselves to forgive, our hearts open to make peace with those things that brought us pain. Withholding forgiveness will only harden our hearts and drive us deeper into a self-imposed prison of anger, bitterness and resentment.

Many of us hold on to the past, reliving the hurt and pain over and over. We're waiting for an admission of guilt or an apology from the other person before offering forgiveness. I've found some conflicts, misunderstandings, and disagreements go unresolved. The other person may never see things our way or feel they have any reason to ask for forgiveness. They go on with their lives, not giving us or the situation a second thought, while we stay stuck. We're unable to fully live life in the present because we're holding on to the past. It's time to forgive and let it go. Farber says, "Forgiveness is more about the forgiver than the forgivee." Forgiveness is not about them; its purpose is to heal the hurt inside of us.

When we forgive, it doesn't make us wrong and them right. Motivational speaker and transformational coach Lisa Nichols says, "forgiveness is not about pardoning people of bad behavior or letting people off the hook." Forgiveness releases us from the past, but not from responsibility. We must hold everyone accountable for their actions and they must deal with the consequences of their decisions.

Forgiveness does not automatically restore trust. Yes, forgiveness is a decision, but trust needs time to rebuild. Some people will disappoint and hurt you repeatedly, then ask, "Please forgive me?" Each offense will probably make it harder for you to forgive, but remember forgiveness is to heal the hurt inside of *you*. However, it's your responsibility to be aware of what's happening around you and determine when it's time to set new boundaries. Sometimes the best thing we can do for ourselves and everyone involved is to love some people from a distance.

Forgiveness is a journey, a process. There may be times when the memory of your painful experience will creep back through your mind and you will have to choose forgiveness again and again until you can completely let go. When you get to the place where you no longer feel the pain and emotions associated with the experience, that's releasing. When you can look past the parts most difficult to live through and understand the lessons within them, that's letting go. When you are at peace with the experience, your choices and actions of the past, that's forgiveness.

Giving thought to forgiveness, ask yourself:

- Are you reliving your past mistakes and poor choices, unable to forgive yourself and move on?
- Did someone close to you hurt and disappoint you, and you're waiting for an apology or admission of guilt before you forgive?
- Have you realized that forgiveness is to heal the hurt inside you, and it may be time to let go?

CHAPTER 6

Loving Me

It had been about fifteen years since I'd seen Robert. We met as kids singing in the church choir. Rob was more interesting than the guys around my neighborhood. I was a city girl while he was from the suburbs zipping around on his minibike, working as a lifeguard during the summer and playing drums with his band on the weekends. Rob was streetwise and accustomed to standing up for himself. Some people thought he was a bit too rough around the edges for a preacher's daughter, but both my parents adored him and so did I.

He was more than just my first boyfriend; he was my friend. Rob listened to me without judgement, no matter what I was talking about. When I had zero confidence in myself, Rob convinced me I could do anything if I tried. We drifted apart, but I often thought about him, especially when times were tough.

Then one day I saw him walking through the parking lot on his way to church. After service it wasn't hard to find him because he was looking for me too. We exchanged numbers and got together later in the week.

Right away it was like old times. Rob and I laughed and talked all night, reminiscing about the old days. The conversation turned to our present-day personal horror stories. My drama was lightweight compared to the heavy load Rob was hauling around. His life spiraled out of control after his Navy service ended. He got caught up in the drug culture of the 1970s and quickly developed a drug addiction. Addiction cost him his job and left him with a criminal record and separated from his wife. He also lost contact with his daughter, Heather. Hearing any of those facts should have sent me running in the opposite direction like my hair was on fire… but it was Robert!

My judgement was clouded by the memory of who he used to be. Rob said he was turning his life around. I believed if anyone could do it, he could, and I wanted to support him through the transition. Everyone deserves a second chance and someone to believe in them.

We quickly became inseparable, talking several times a day and spending all our free time together. However, when I didn't hear from him for a day or two, I didn't need to be a rocket scientist to figure out where he was. Every time he'd resurface with empty pockets, full of remorse and promising it would never happen again. But it always happened again. We'd talk, meaning I lectured him on what he already knew—that his getting high even occasionally had serious consequences.

Then I'd give him just enough carfare to get back and forth to work until his next payday. I really thought I was helping, but without realizing it I was enabling his behavior by not allowing him to face the full effects of his actions. I'd talk to him about drug programs, professional counseling, anything to help him, but Rob insisted on dealing with his problem "his way," which clearly wasn't working.

I was in over my head; I knew nothing about dealing with an addict. I didn't see the addict I saw Robert; I worried what would happen if I wasn't there. Then he started disappearing more frequently and missing work too. Things were getting out of control. It felt like I was trying to harness a runaway train. I had to accept Rob wasn't ready for change, and to save my sanity, I stepped away.

Life has a way of zooming by when you're not paying attention. When Rob finally called, I realized it had been quite a while since we spoke. He wanted to meet for dinner. I was hesitant at first, but he assured me I had nothing to worry about; he just wanted to talk.

My heart skipped a beat when I caught a glimpse of him from across the street. I'd forgotten how handsome he was and without him saying a word, I knew the Rob I fell in love with was back. The good news: he had been drug-free for a few years. The bad news: he lost everything before accepting he couldn't get sober and stay sober his way. He went through an intense residential drug treatment program and continued with an outpatient program that lasted a year. Now he was back in the workforce full time and doing some catering on the side. Most importantly his daughter was back in his life.

Rob apologized for the drama he brought into my life. It embarrassed him how he showed up last time, that's why he took so long reaching out to me. He missed our talks and wonder if we could just be friends again. I was genuinely happy for him, and I missed my friend too, so I said yes. And just like that, two friends were back together again, but this time without the chaos and drama. Our friendship turned into a commitment, and we made it official two years later. His daughter Heather was my maid of honor, and Derek was Rob's best man.

Our marriage was the fairytale ending to our story. However, the thought was always in the back of my mind, because of his history, what if his sobriety doesn't last? A few years into our marriage, Rob broke his foot in an accident at work. After surgery, his doctor prescribed opioid pain medication. For a recovering addict, a controlled substance, even when prescribed, can be dangerous. The doctors assured me everything would be okay, and it was.

However, an unrelated second surgery months later, with more pain meds, ushered in a life I could never have imagined. You can stand on the sidelines watching a roller coaster go around and around all day long, but it doesn't compare to being strapped in the front seat taking those steep climbs and low plunges for yourself. Life with Rob became a roller coaster ride on steroids. Every time I thought it couldn't get worse, it got worse.

One Sunday evening I was already in bed when I heard his keys in the door. It was a payday weekend; I hadn't seen him since he left for work Friday morning. Rob would go up to Harlem or out on Long Island when he wanted to get high, keeping that part of his life far away from home. Still, I was furious with him because he knew the slippery slope he was on. We'd been down this road before and we both knew how the story would end.

Rob stood in the doorway for a while before entering our bedroom. Falling on his knees at the side of the bed, he began sobbing, "I'm sorry, I'm sorry… Daddy's watch."

In the darkened room, there was just enough light from the hallway to see my father's watch was missing from its usual place on Rob's dresser. My sister and I gave him the watch when Daddy passed away. He had grown very close to my dad and I know he cherished the watch. But drugs will make you do the unthinkable. Through clenched teeth I said, "Get it back."

I didn't think about what he might have to do to retrieve the watch. At that moment I really didn't care, I just wanted things back the way they were. There was no conversation in the house for the next two weeks; on payday the watch was back in its spot, but it didn't restore the brokenness between us.

When I was his girlfriend, I could walk away, but now as his wife, how would I deal with him being out of control? Arguing and fighting had no effect on the situation. Ignoring it, hoping he'd come to his senses, was not the solution either. I realized that the longer I did nothing, the longer I was condoning his bad behavior and putting myself in danger. I gave him an ultimatum: Get help or I'm out. I drew my line in the sand—he crossed it. I drew another line—he crossed that too. Over and over, chance after chance. I was trying to avoid the inevitable. All my time, energy and emotions were focused on him realizing what was at stake and changing his reckless behavior. All the while I was losing myself and fearful if he continued the end results may be a financial disaster, jail or death. I felt I had no options left.

Sitting in the lawyer's office, I could barely see where to place my signature on the divorce papers through the tears filling my eyes. "Mrs. Brown are you sure this is what you want to do?" the lawyer asked. Slowly I nodded my head yes; afraid if I spoke, my voice would betray the decision I'd made to end the marriage. I thought divorce would make the pain go away.

Divorce is the death of a relationship, but few will acknowledge the depth of your loss or give you the time to grieve. People will say, "Good riddance to bad rubbish," then encourage you to get over it as quickly as possible. Divorce isn't one of those occasions when people bring over a covered dish and sit and chat. It was difficult dealing with the mix of emotions because Rob wasn't a bad person, and I still loved him.

Don't get me wrong, I was angry as hell at him for destroying what we had together, but I was angrier at myself for a second failed marriage. I tried placing all the blame on my ex-husbands. Then I remembered what one of the former pastors of my church, Rev. Albert D. Tyson, used to say: "Be careful when you point your finger at someone because there are three fingers pointing back at you." I was the common factor in both marriages. How did I fail at marriage two times? What was wrong with me?

By this time in my life, I was no stranger to depression. I wasn't sure if it was the cause or effect of poor choices, low self-esteem, or stuffing my real feelings down. Either way, I landed in a dark emotional hole. There were times the depression was so debilitating I had no energy or desire to do anything other than crawl into bed, pull the covers over my head and cry, hoping I'd fall asleep. Sleep was my way to escape feelings of sadness and hopelessness.

Divorce number two may have triggered the onset of this round of depression, but it was my long list of failures and disappointments playing in my mind that kept me down. I believed that no matter what; something predestined me to failure. Happiness and a normal life would always be just beyond my reach. What sense did it make to keep trying when nothing good ever happened for me? Thoughts of ending the pain by ending my life floated around in my head.

Suicide was never my goal; I was way too big a coward to kill myself. I just didn't want to hurt anymore. I didn't want to feel like a failure anymore, and I grow tired of the tears. I thought if I could go to sleep and never wake up, it would all go away.

I had pushed Rob relentlessly to get professional help for his addiction, but it never occurred to me that I needed help with my own issues. Depression was a way of life for me; I didn't think I could do anything about it. It usually came in waves; subsiding long enough for me to pull myself together. But not this time. Instead of having space between episodes, this time the depression hovered over me like a deep dense fog, limiting my ability to function sensibly. I wasn't eating or sleeping. My thoughts and emotions weren't rational. The guilt and embarrassment I felt from facing a second divorce was consuming me. I knew I had to pull myself together, but I couldn't do it on my own.

Self-Love

My employer offered an assistance program, which included counseling with a licensed mental health professional. I made an appointment to get help. My counselor, Nicole, started our first session with a simple enough question: "Why are you here?"

I thought I knew why I came, but somehow it was a difficult question to answer. I could hear myself rambling on and on. I wondered if Nicole could make any sense of what I was trying to say. By the end of our first session, Nicole told me depression was an issue and gaining tools to cope would be my priority number one.

Through our discussions and the pamphlets Nicole gave me to read, I learned that depression is a common and sometimes debilitating mood disorder. Depression affects how you feel, think, and function in the world. It's not the same as being a little down or feeling sad now and then. In most cases, you can't shake it off or pray it away. You cannot hide from it; you must deal with depression head on. There are people that may need medication to regulate their mood, but behavioral changes are effective for others.

Nicole recommended a few things for me, and physical exercise was one suggestion. She didn't advice long, strenuous workouts at a gym, just a simple walk around the neighborhood to get my body moving. She also encouraged me to focus on the positive things in my life and write them down. I know these may sound overly simplistic, but the results proved their value. As I continued to work with Nicole slowly, I felt the depression lift.

Every other week for the next few months, I met with Nicole. We talked about my life and my relationships. During one session Nicole interrupted me to say, "Pegi, you deserve love" she paused then continued "but first you must learn to love yourself" I didn't understand her. For me, self-love was a negative. It meant a person was vain or a narcissist.

That's not what she meant at all. Nicole explained self-love reflects how you value yourself. It's when you care enough to make your well-being a top priority.

Self-love means being as concerned about your own needs being met as you are with meeting the needs of others. Nicole pointed out the Bible says "… love your neighbor as yourself." It doesn't say to love your neighbor more than yourself. I realized my idea of love was flipped upside down and backwards. I was trying to earn love and loyalty through sacrifice and selflessness because I didn't value myself. I tolerated bad behavior, gave far more than I ever received, and I stayed in relationships long past their expiration date because I didn't think I was worth anything better.

It was time to establish a loving relationship with myself. First, I wrote a list of all my good qualities, gifts and talents and a list of my likes and dislikes. Then, I started jotting down anytime someone gave me a compliment no matter how small; I wanted to see what others saw in me. I needed to get to know myself from the inside out. I was ready to love myself for my uniqueness. The biggest step of all was putting self-care and self-love on the top of my priority list.

Loving me meant letting go of the guilt and shame associated with facing a second divorce. I had to give up my victim story that made him the villain because of his poor choices. I accepted that I'd made poor choices too, and that didn't make either of us bad people. It allowed room in my heart to first love myself and then find compassion for another human being dealing with his own issues. Rob eventually found what he needed to end his destructive behavior and remained sober for the last ten plus years of his life.

One day, sitting in Nicole's office just thinking about how far I'd come, the tears flowed non-stop. These tears differed from the ones I'd shed in the beginning, from a place of hurt and pain. Now my tears were from understanding my value and worth. I didn't have to put myself at the bottom of my priority list or sacrifice my sanity to earn love. I learned that I deserved love, and I started by loving myself.

When we love ourselves, we have so much more to give to others. Take a few moments to consider these questions:

- Does your life reflect your value and worth?
- How do you show self-love in your life?
- Are you at the top of your priority list? If not, why not?

CHAPTER 7

Guarding My Mind

Attending college for the first time at age fifty-eight challenged my long-held belief that I wasn't smart enough. From day one my grades were through the roof. This should have been enough to convince me that I was more than capable of handling the work, but that old, old story in my head wouldn't stop.

Every semester began with the same thoughts I heard all my life: "You're not smart enough," "You're in over your head," plus a newcomer: "You're too old to learn something new." It usually took completing a few class assignments before I felt comfortable and the negative chatter faded to the background. Then came statistics. All the City University of New York schools require at least one college-level math course to graduate, regardless of your major. After struggling with the remedial algebra class I had to take because I didn't have it in high school, I wanted to stay as far away as possible from anything that resembled algebra, including geometry and trigonometry. Although I heard a few horror stories, statistics still seemed like the best choice.

Good thing I didn't take that class my first semester, or there never would have been a second semester for me. With only three classes left before graduation, it was time to face the music and register for the class. My plan was to do whatever it took to make it through.

They say, "throw enough mud against the wall, and some will stick." I threw everything I could at statistics. I spent hours in the math clinic, paid a tutor out of pocket, used an online math tutoring service, I even bought and read *Statistics for Dummies*. I was desperate. Each tactic helped a little; I had minor breakthroughs here and there, but I wasn't mastering enough of the concepts or progressing fast enough to keep up with the class. The negative conversation in my head went into overdrive, drowning out any thought I'd succeed. After another session in the math clinic with a professor who I'm convinced was speaking a secret code only math wizards understood, I knew I would fail. It was hopeless. Walking toward my car, I tried coming up with another way around it, but my only option seemed to be to quit—walk away from the whole thing. There was no reason for a degree at this point in my life. It wouldn't help with my present position, and I wasn't planning on switching careers now. I would retire in a few years.

From the day I started college, I expected eventually I'd hit a brick wall that would confirm I didn't belong in school. I guess this was it. Then I questioned the value of all my accomplishments while at LaGuardia. Did any of it matter if I couldn't pass statistics? I got in my car and sat a long time, then made my decision. I didn't need this stress—I QUIT!!!

What a feeling of relief—immediately the pressure was off. I could breathe again. I didn't have to worry about the class, homework, or finals anymore. I was free. I headed home.

As usual, the Long Island Expressway was bumper to bumper. Sitting in traffic, I thought about how my life had changed since entering college. College challenged me to think critically by gathering information, analyzing it, and drawing my conclusion based on what I found to be true—not someone else's opinion. I took introductory classes in linguistics, sociology, physiology, and philosophy—all subjects that intimidated me at first, but I found fascinating and broadened my view of the world. I realized how much I enjoyed learning new things.

Despite dyslexia, I had racked up major academic accomplishments that only a few years earlier I never could have imagined possible, like making the Dean's List. I had also joined the Phi Theta Kappa Honor Society, which Derek had to explain to me was a pretty big deal—especially my Golden Key status. That was an even bigger deal. I learned a new level of discipline and perseverance when I stayed up all night until my eyeballs were on fire, writing papers and studying for finals. So many other things went through my mind that had boosted my self-confidence and showed me success isn't limited to the naturally smart and gifted. It's for the determined as well. For me, college was never about getting a better job; it was about following my dream and proving to myself I could do it.

By the time I pulled into my garage I had a change of heart. Quitting was not an option anymore. No way I would let my hard work and all the challenges I'd overcome go down the tubes because of one subject. If I walked away now, I'd be allowing the negative chatter in my head to rob me of my dreams. I decided to fight to the finish against the negative conversation going on in my mind.

Determined to graduate on time, I needed a new plan to deal with statistics and my negative thoughts. Whenever I heard *you can't* in my mind, "you can" came out of my mouth. Those moments when I felt overwhelmed, I reminded myself of all the things I had already accomplished. I wish I could say something clicked in my brain and the class miraculously got easier, but that's not what happened. Still, I hung in there and passed the class. And I proudly walked across the Madison Square Garden stage as the oldest LAGCC graduate in the class of 2015.

What Are You Thinking?

Do you ever think about what you're thinking about? What are you saying to yourself all day long? Is your inner conversation filled with words that empower and encourage you to move in the direction of your dreams? Or is it filled with negativity, holding you back from achieving success? Most of us are unaware of the chatter playing in the background of our minds or how it affects our lives.

According to the National Science Foundation, the average human mind has between 12,000 and 60,000 thoughts each day. They found that 95% are the same thoughts we had the day before, and 80% of those are negative. Thoughts repeated day after day will eventually become our beliefs. Beliefs determine our mindset, and our mindset determines the results that show up in our lives.

Our mindset functions like the set-point on a thermostat. If the temperature falls below the set-point, the heat comes on. When the temperature rises above the set-point, the thermostat automatically turns the heat off and the temperature falls until it's below the set-point again. The goal is to keep the temperature within the parameters of the set-point. Our mindset is the set-point of our lives. It limits us to fit within the parameters of what we believe to be possible for us. No matter how daring we may be, we'll eventually snap back like a rubber band to remain in alignment with our mindset. To get different results, we must adjust our mindset by guarding our mind.

If you want to know the conversation going on in the background of your mind, listen to the words coming out of your mouth. Our words reflect our thoughts. Thoughts like "I'm so stupid," "I can't do anything right," "I'll never (fill in the blank...)" reinforce the negative view we have of ourselves, limiting our capacity to grow and setting us up to fail. If you want a different outcome, choose a different conversation.

Be vigilant about who you allow to enter your inner circle. Their thoughts can infiltrate your thoughts without you noticing. Author and motivational speaker Jim Rohn said, "You are the average of the five people you spend the most time with." If your friends are positive, you'll be positive, but if they're negative—well, you get the picture.

It's human nature to want to fit in with the crowd, but in the words of Dr. Seuss, "Why fit in when you were born to stand out?" Fitting in with people who have no dreams or goals of their own will stifle you. I'm not suggesting you dump your friends, un-friend them on social media, or block their numbers. But you might want to do a little mindset check. Are their conversations uplifting and inspiring, encouraging you to be your best? Or do they drag you down with constant complaining and negativity?

I have a friend I've learned to love from a distance because her conversation leaves me drained. I feel a physical heaviness after spending time with her, either on the phone or in person. She's still my friend, but my well-being is too important to have her as part of my inner circle where her negative talk might penetrate my mind.

It's not enough to know where the negative thoughts originate. You must be proactive in keeping them out in the first place by saturating your mind with positive, encouraging words that will inspire you. And surround yourself with people that will not only lift you up but challenge you to be your best.

Erasing the Negative

Before your life can change, your thinking must change. If you allow negative chatter to run unchecked through your mind, it will show up in your life. It's impossible to think negative and live positive. You must challenge your thoughts, examine them to see if they are the truth or just a lie you've repeated so often that you believe it's true. Below is an exercise I was first introduced to at a personal development conference. I did a little research and found it's a practice often used in cognitive behavior therapy, but I just think it's a really cool way to erase the negative conversation playing in the background of your mind. And what's great is whenever you feel the negative crowding out the positive you can go through the exercise again.

Begin by writing down every negative thought that comes to mind, every doubt and fear that holds you back from living the life of your dreams. Using a pencil or pen with blue or black ink jot down every lie you tell yourself that keeps you from reaching for success. Leave three lines blank between each of the negative thoughts or lies that you wrote down. If you can't think of what to write down consider different areas of your life where negative thoughts crop up: health and wellness, finance, career, relationships, spirituality, etc. Take your time with this. The more you write down the better. If you run out of space, add more paper—keep writing until you run out of lies. It probably won't feel good digging up all the negativity, but don't let that scare you or stop you. You're about to disrupt the lies that are blocking you.

Next take a different color pen…my preference is red ink because it really stands out. On the blank lines below each lie write down the truth, phrased as a positive statement—even if you can't believe it yet. For some lies you may not know what the truth looks like for you, but this is an opportunity to explore what your new story will be. For example, one of your lies might be: *I'll never be able to reach this goal.* Some truths you could say to counteract these thoughts might include: *I have what it takes to achieve my goals!* This may be a challenge, and it will take time, but it's necessary to do in order to break through the negative thoughts that have prevented you from achieving success.

Now, every day for the next week, read the lie and then read the truth.

On the seventh day, erase or cross out all the lies. Only the truth in contrasting ink will remain. Whenever the negative thought pops into your head, a positive statement of truth will be attached to it.

This is not only a great process to expose the negative chatter in the background of your mind, but you have just written positive affirmations customized for you. You can use them daily to guard your mind.

CHAPTER 8

From Caterpillar to Butterfly

To become a butterfly, the caterpillar gives up the life it once knew. It transforms into something completely different, not just a better caterpillar. A metamorphosis occurs, a radical change in which the caterpillar sheds the old to make way for the next chapter of life. After the transformation takes place, it has the struggle of a lifetime to break free, emerging as a magnificent butterfly.

To break into my next chapter, I felt I needed a metamorphosis. A radical change in both my thinking and my actions would be necessary before the new version of Pegi could emerge.

Transformation is never about what we leave behind or even the finished product; it's about what happens on the journey. As exciting as it was to begin my next chapter, I worried that I had waited too late. Whenever I thought of the years I'd wasted trapped in my world of self-doubt and fear, I wondered if at this age, change was even possible. Still, I couldn't allow my past insecurities to hold my future hostage any longer. I had to do whatever it took to break free and step into my next chapter a changed woman.

I was one hundred percent committed to taking action. The problem was, I had no clue what to do next. Transforming our lives wasn't exactly a topic of conversation when I got together with my girlfriends. We talked about changing jobs, changing hair styles or even changing men, but transforming our lives never came up. If I would see change, I'd have to figure this out on my own.

With a sense of urgency, I started changing how I approached life. "Yes" became my mantra. I said yes to life. No hiding out or excuses any more—I was all in, ready to take on life and live it to the fullest. I began acting like a new and improved Pegi, even though I didn't feel new and improved on the inside yet. When the music played, I wouldn't just dance in my seat anymore. I hit the dance floor ready to do my thing regardless of who was watching. Every invitation got a yes response. Sometimes I dove in so fast I surprised myself, but I was making up for lost time.

There were so many things I wanted to accomplish, places I wanted to go, and experiences I wanted to have. I took a yellow legal pad and started creating a list. Nothing was too extreme to make my list. If I thought about it, I wrote it down. Some people might refer to this as a bucket list, as in Things to Do Before I Kick the Bucket. Not me. Why would I want to think about dying before I really lived? Instead, I called it my wish list. Over time, I expanded my list to include pictures, positive quotes, and scriptures. I put it all in a book and called it my dream book. Every day during my devotional time, then again right before bed, I looked at my book for inspiration and motivation to keep going.

It was fun and exciting, experiencing new things, accomplishing new goals. With each accomplishment my confidence grew; encouraging me to try bigger, more challenging things next time. Learning to swim had been on my mind for years, so I decided now was the time. I'm no authority on how the Law of Attraction works, but I've learned that being crystal clear on what you want is an important part. It's amazing what can happen when you focus your attention on the things you desire. Solutions to problems seem to appear out of nowhere; answers rise to the forefront of your thoughts. It's not magic—you must still put in the effort when the opportunity shows itself.

Within days of deciding to take up swimming, the Queens College summer brochure arrived in my mailbox. I've lived a half block from Queens College since 1993. I had neither received a brochure from them before nor have I received one since, but that one brochure arrived right on time. The school offered an adult beginners swimming course starting the next week. There was no time for hemming and hawing about it. *Yes!* I signed up.

And on that first day, as I stepped out of the locker room, my legs felt like two giant lead pipes. My flip-flops seemed glued to the floor as I struggled to walk along the side of the pool deck. To say I was nervous would be an enormous understatement. It terrified me. Groups of small children filled the pool, each one bobbling along to the direction of their instructors. Along the wall were benches filled with others awaiting their turn in the water. A quick glance around told me there wasn't anyone even close to my age in sight.

Fear rose inside of me as my mind raced from one thought to another. All thoughts converged on the same idea: how the hell could I escape this uncomfortable situation? What started as a declaration of my commitment to live life to the fullest, at this point, seemed awfully foolish. What in the world was I thinking, trying to accomplish at fifty-six something most people learn in childhood?

A shout interrupted my thoughts. "Hey-hey!"

I hadn't noticed when I entered, but this pool was in the facility where the Queens College swim team competed. There were quite a few people sitting in the stands behind me; some watching their children while others were getting ready for a meet that would start when lessons were over. *Terrific—now I have an audience watching me make a fool of myself,* I thought.

"Hey-hey!" There it was again.

Now, looking in the noise's direction, I saw a woman waving her arms and gesturing towards me. Without my glasses, I couldn't tell if she was someone I knew. I turned to see whose attention she was trying to get. "Hey, Lady! Yes, you." She was pointing at me. "If you can do it, I know I can too!" She gave me a thumbs up. My face broke into a big Kool-Aid grin as my hand, as though on autopilot, raised high in the air to return her thumbs up. Unaware of what she had done, a total stranger had given me the encouragement I needed to fight through my fears and take my place alongside the other adult students in the pool; all of whom were half my age. As I inspired her, she confirmed for me I was on the right track and it wasn't too late.

Every new adventure presented fresh challenges, but when I achieved each small goal that led to a bigger one, my self-confidence and self-esteem soared. As a bonus, I was inspiring others—sometimes total strangers, like the lady at the pool. When I began my journey, I never imagined that because I was courageous enough to step from the sidelines and live my life, it would encourage others to do the same. That inspired and motivated me even more.

As much as I enjoyed finally living life, I felt something was missing. For this fresh approach to life to be lasting, and for me to be open to change at even higher levels, it would require more than checking items off a to-do list. I thought back to when I first became a Mary Kay Consultant. As a single mom, making ends meet was always a challenge. Selling Mary Kay Cosmetics was something I could do to make money and still be home with Derek. My sales director, Juanita Johnson Farnum often spoke on personal development topics at our sales meeting and encourage me to read books on the subject. Mary Kay became much more than a money-making opportunity. Focusing on personal development sharply improved my confidence and thus my sales. So, seeing the improvement, I applied some of the same techniques to my transformational journey.

Personal development comprises of various elements. It improves self-awareness, develop talents and uncover potential, enhance the quality of your life and contribute to the realization of your dreams. It's about investing in yourself to experience life at the highest level of personal fulfilment. Rather than hoping and wishing for change, you become proactive in creating the best version of yourself while living the life of your dreams. You put in the work daily to transform every area of your life. You may fall short at times, but you will experience a richer, more rewarding life when you commit yourself to stepping onto the never-ending road to personal development. And when disappointments come, as they often do, you develop the bounce-back tools to overcome and keep going.

Some people confuse personal development and growth with the New Age movement, metaphysical philosophy, or Eastern religious practices. They feel it's a rejection of reliance on their Divine Creator… but that's not true. Improving your life experience through personal development doesn't exclude your relationship with God. Rather, it enhances it.

To move forward, you must take responsibility for where you are today… giving up all excuses or victim stories for how you got there. A major component of personal development is self-awareness. Knowing your core values, confident in your beliefs, and sure of the purpose you are here is more important than chasing the latest trend, or someone else's dream. Being clear and focusing on what you want to achieve in life will keep you motivated; and during the tough times provide the resilience to get back up and keep going. Now that's the stuff I was looking for.

I took a stroll down the aisles of the local bookstore and found authors like Jack Canfield, Valerie Burton, John Maxwell, Napoleon

Hill, Lisa Nichols, and many others. They became my mentors in my head, anyway. Audiobooks became my best friends and my car became my personal development sanctuary on wheels.

The books and tapes were great. They kept me engaged and focused on my plan of becoming a better me. And one day while surfing the internet I stumbled across a women's empowerment conference in Reston, Virginia, just outside the Washington, D. C. area. As the Buddhist proverb goes, "When the student is ready, the teacher will appear." It seemed like just the thing I needed to enhance what I was already doing on my own. I wanted to go. I didn't discuss it with anyone or seek a consensus on whether this was a good idea. This was about me. It was my mission—no one else got a vote. It was time to break out of the cocoon and take a bold step towards my next chapter.

I traveled for the first time out-of-town by myself.

Walking into the ballroom of the hotel where the conference was being held, I didn't know what to expect. Who would be there? Would I get what I came looking for? Or would it be a bunch of women sitting around barefoot, burning candles and reading tea leaves?

When I saw women from every corner of the world around me, each on their individual journeys of personal empowerment, my fears subsided. There were women of every imaginable background. Entrepreneurs, college professors, ministers, housewives, CEOs, founders of nonprofits, doctors, authors, speakers, young women just starting out, and mature women on the path to retirement looking for what's next. Many of these women had overcome tremendous obstacles: financial loss, divorce, death of a loved one, lay-offs, career changes, and business failures. Some had survived physical, emotional, or sexual abuse. So many were willing to share their stories to encourage one another and give each other hope. And it wasn't all doom and gloom. Some of these women were superstars in their field. They were successful in business, community, and ministry, and were there to recharge their battery and get a boost to the next level.

My greatest takeaways from the weekend was that everyone has fears and doubts, and when you don't allow them to stop you from pursuing your dreams, you will accomplish extraordinary things. Even when it seems hopeless, and you are ready to give in, hold on—your breakthrough could be right around the corner. One speaker said, "You will make mistakes. It's inevitable; you're only human. But don't be so hard on yourself. Give yourself a hundred second chances. And when you get to ninety-nine, hit the reset button and start over again."

It was encouraging to know my age didn't matter, when I started didn't matter, my financial status or educational background didn't matter. The only thing that mattered was my willingness to give it my best and never give up.

When I got home, I was on fire. More than ever, I was determined to change my life. Every step-by-step guide, book, CD, video, online course, seminar, or workshop promoted at the conference I was ready to try. If I could get my hands on it, I wanted to absorb it all overnight… but it doesn't work like that. Personal development is an ongoing process. It's not something you can do once and finish. Some things you will understand and be able to integrate into your life right away and others will take time. And no single "Ten Steps to a New You!" method works for everybody.

You must find what makes the most sense for you and follow that path. If you commit and stay the course, when you look back you will see the growth. Think of climbing a staircase, each step prepares you for the next, but if you stop halfway, you will never know how beautiful it is at the top.

I absolutely wanted something different in my life. You've heard the saying "If you want something different you have to do something different." Well, that meant I had to give up doing the same old thing the same old way. Through my prayer and meditation time, readings, self-reflection, and personal development exercises, a vision for my life emerged.

Having a vision differs from setting goals. Goals are an important part of getting us where we want to go. They are our to-do list, our business plan, our step-by-step road map. Vision, on the other hand, is the overall reason we do what we do. Vision defines who we want to be, what we want to be known for, what the world will look like because of our contribution. Our vision is a picture of our future. Our vision must be in alignment with our core values, our beliefs, and our purpose in life.

When I started my journey, I wasn't sure what I was doing. I was making it up as I went along. All I knew was *I wanted something different*. Some things worked while others did not. The changes that worked resulted in great outcomes. The changes that didn't work resulted in valuable lessons and the courage to keep on trying. Then one day I noticed a shift in the way I saw the world and how the world was seeing me. The cocoon was slipping away, my metamorphosis was occurring, and I was heading into my next chapter.

Forming Your Vision

Your vision is the *big picture* view of your life. It provides a framework for how you will show up in the world. One way to develop your vision is to imagine life through the eyes of your future self. Try this exercise:

- Imagine your older self, perhaps twenty years out, or even just five years from now.
- You're relaxing in your favorite chair, sipping a glass of wine or a cup of herbal tea.
- You're reflecting on your life and thinking about the most important accomplishments or experiences you've had to this point.
- What would you like to be looking back on?
- What are the highlights you'd enjoy reliving?

- Whose life have you touched?
- What difference have you made?
- What are you most proud of?
- What made your heart sing? Or satisfied your soul?
- How have you fulfilled your life purpose?
- How are you using your unique gifts (humor, kindness, creativity, etc.)?
- What will your legacy be?

Thinking about these questions can help you tune into what really matters to you. Knowing what really matters is important in forming a vision that will guide you toward your next chapter and beyond.

Next Chapter

Through the pages of this book I've shared stories of mistakes I've made, and lessons I learned, that together shaped my life and pointed me toward my next chapter. Revisiting some of these memories was difficult, but I believe when we dare to share our stories, we give each other hope. Although your path may differ from mine, it is my hope and prayer that while reading my story, something nudged you to look at your own life. Don't look back through eyes of judgement or hold yourself hostage to the mistakes of the past. Instead, find the lessons you can use to propel you forward into your next chapter.

You may think, as I did when I started on this journey, that it's too late or the time has passed for you to try something new. That's just not true. One major lesson I've learned is that it's never too late. I met a woman at an event who told me she walked down the aisle as a first-time bride at seventy years old, fulfilling a lifelong dream. Another woman I know learned to drive at fifty-five, and one went skiing for the first time in her sixties. Dorothy Steel is another amazing example that it's never too late. At ninety-two years old, Ms. Steel played a tribal elder in Marvel's 2018 blockbuster hit *Black Panther*.

She only began her professional acting career at eighty-eight years old. If you were fortunate enough to wake up this morning, there is still something meaningful for you to accomplish in your life.

Don't allow your past to hold you back from creating an amazing future. Let go of the stories of who you used to be and step into the person you were created to become. Forgive those who may have hurt you, more important than that, forgive yourself and move on. Learn to love yourself just as you are. You are on the way to becoming a new and improved version of yourself. Create a fresh vision for your life and commit to making your next chapter your best chapter!

Next Steps (Next Chapter!) for You

To live a balanced and successful next chapter, start by deciding what you want to achieve in the following seven areas: work and career, finances, recreation and free time, health and fitness, relationships, personal goals, and contributions to the larger community. Grab paper and a pen and create your dream list.

- Think about what you would do if you knew you couldn't fail. Don't hold back. Nothing is off limits. It's your list—for your eyes only. A magnificent way to start is to list thirty things you want to do, thirty things you want to have, and thirty things you want to become. Don't worry if you can't finish your list in one sitting. It's something you can come back to again and again.
- Now select three items from your list to focus on right away. One item should be achievable in a week, one in a month and the others can take six to twelve months to complete.
- For each item make a plan to get the job done. Then, act.

Congratulations! You are on your way to your next chapter. Stay encouraged and be blessed.

Suggested Reading for Next Chapter Living

Become a Better You:7 Keys to Improving Your Live Every Day by Joel Osteen (Free Press, 2007)

Dream It. Pin It. Live It.: Make Vision Boards Work For You by Terri Savelle Foy (Terri Savelle Foy Ministries, 2015)

How to Succeed at Being Yourself: Finding the Confidence to Fulfill Your Destiny by Joyce Meyer (Harrison House, 1999)

If Life is a Game, These are the Rules: Ten Rules for Being Human by Cherie Carter-Scott (Harmony, 1999)

No Matter What! 9 Steps to Living the Life You Love by Lisa Nichols (Grand Central Life & Style 2011)

The Four Agreements: A Practical Guide to Personal Freedom by Don Miguel Ruiz (Amber – Allen Publishing, 2018)

The Success Principles: How to Get From Where You are to Where you Want to Be by Jack Canfield (Element Books, 2005)

Where Will You Go from Here?: Moving Forward When Life Doesn't Go as Planned by Valorie Burton (Waterbrook, 2011)

Acknowledgements

An ancient African proverb says, "It takes a whole village to raise a child." So it was in creating this project. It was my vision, but it was the continued encouragement and support of my loving community that brought this book into existence I am eternally grateful to:

My developmental editor Susan Herman for organizing my thoughts and turning them into a viable manuscript. Then challenging me to go deeper.

My copy editor Carolyn Scavella for putting the finishing touches on this project. She believed in my vision when it was still just a dream and encouraged me to go for it.

My Mary Kay Sales Director, Juanita Johnson Farnum for introducing me to personal development and inspiring me to set big goals.

My niece Jackie Crane for her enthusiasm about my vision and reminding me when I got discouraged that things would look better in the morning.

My sister-friends Mary Diakite and Carol Miller for giving me space to be my authentic self. Both enthusiastic champions of my vision and urging me to make my best even better.

My sister, Rev. Beryl "Cooki" Days for our shared life experience and the ability to laugh through things only we can understand.

My Father, Rev. John B. Days for never giving up on me and teaching me the importance of a solid spiritual foundation.

My cousins, Theresa Redford, Cecelia Crane, Deborah Jordan, for growing up surrounded by love and laughter. Gone way too soon, they've inspired me to live my next chapter in their honor.

My Video Tuesday Facebook Community for receiving my chats and sometimes ramblings, convincing me my message was worth sharing.

The attendees of my first "It's Your Time" Women's Empowerment Conference insisting I have my book available next time we meet.

And finally, to my former husband Robert Allen Brown Jr. his love and friendship last beyond the end of our marriage. He always encouraged me to write, and that's exactly what I did.

…but one thing I do, **forgetting those things** which are **behind** and reaching forward to **those things** which are ahead.

Philippians 3:13 NKJV

About the Author

Pegi Ivery Brown is an inspirational speaker, author, and certified personal coach. In her down-to-earth style, Pegi shares her message that "it's never too late" through empowerment workshops, personal development sessions, and weekly inspirational videos posted to social media. She is the founder and executive director of Ivery Brown, LLC, a company on a mission to inspire and encourage mature women to step confidently into their next chapter. Pegi is a member of the International Coach Federation and received certification in Personal Development Coaching from the CaPP Institute, Atlanta GA. She graduated with honors from LaGuardia Community College of the City University of New York, at age sixty-two. A native New Yorker, Pegi lives in Kew Gardens Hills, New York.

Are you ready for
Next Chapter Living?

It will require you to take bold and courageous action steps to create a new and improved you.

The good news, it's never too late, and you do not have to go it alone. Our goal is to support you on your journey.

To stay inspired, motivated and empowered
visit us at www.IveryBrown.com
for bonus resources designed just for you.

To learn more about Pegi Ivery Brown's upcoming workshops, seminars, individual/group coaching sessions or to book her for a speaking engagement email info@iverybrown.com

Dream List

1. _____
2. _____
3. _____
4. _____
5. _____
6. _____
7. _____
8. _____
9. _____
10. _____
11. _____
12. _____
13. _____
14. _____
15. _____
16. _____
17. _____
18. _____
19. _____
20. _____
21. _____
22. _____
23. _____
24. _____
25. _____

Dream List

26. _____

27. _____

28. _____

29. _____

30. _____

31. _____

32. _____

33. _____

34. _____

35. _____

36. _____

37. _____

38. _____

39. _____

40. _____

41. _____

42. _____

43. _____

44. _____

45. _____

46. _____

47. _____

48. _____

49. _____

50. _____

Dream List

51. _____

52. _____

53. _____

54. _____

55. _____

56. _____

57. _____

58. _____

59. _____

60. _____

61. _____

62. _____

63. _____

64. _____

65. _____

66. _____

67. _____

68. _____

69. _____

70. _____

71. _____

72. _____

73. _____

74. _____

75. _____

Dream List

76. _____

77. _____

78. _____

79. _____

80. _____

81. _____

82. _____

83. _____

84. _____

85. _____

86. _____

87. _____

88. _____

89. _____

90. _____

91. _____

92. _____

93. _____

94. _____

95. _____

96. _____

97. _____

98. _____

99. _____

100. _____

Action Plan

Short-Range Goal _____

    Plan _____

_____

_____

_____

_____

Date Accomplished _____

Mid-Range Goal _____

    Plan _____

_____

_____

_____

_____

Date Accomplished _____

Long-Range Goal _____

    Plan _____

_____

_____

_____

_____

Date Accomplished _____

Journal

_____

_____

_____

_____

_____

_____

_____

_____

_____

_____

_____

_____

_____

_____

_____

_____

_____

_____

_____

_____

_____

_____

_____

_____

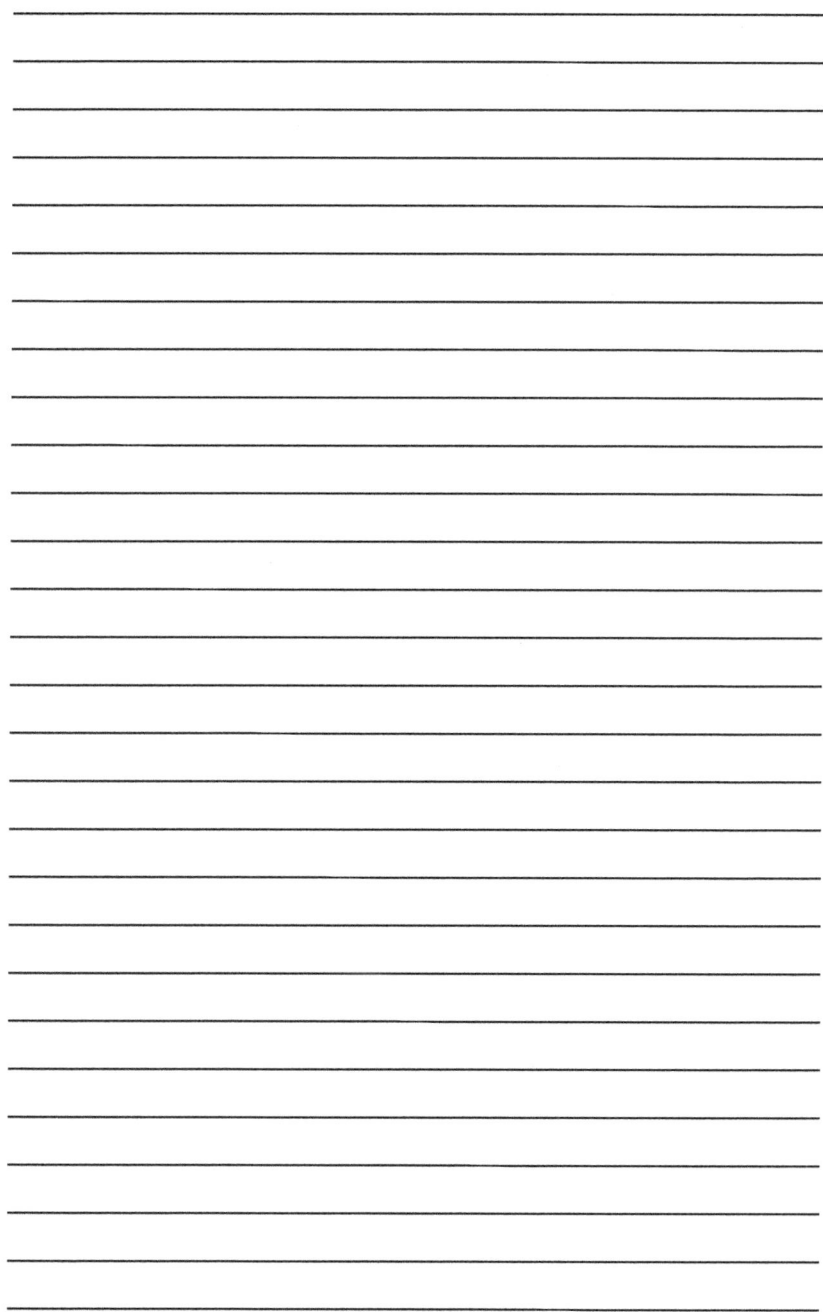

www.ingramcontent.com/pod-product-compliance
Lightning Source LLC
LaVergne TN
LVHW091203080426
835509LV00006B/802